THE BONE LADDER

THE BONE LADDER

ROSEMARY SULLIVAN

BLACK MOSS PRESS
2000

Published by Black Moss Press at 2450 Byng Road, Windsor, Ontaario, N8W
3E8. Canada. Black Moss books are distributed in Canada and the U.S. by
Firefly Books. All orders should be directed there.

Black Moss would like to acknowledge the Canada Council for the Arts for
its publishing program. Also thanks to the Ontario Arts Council for its assis-
tance this year.

Cataloguing in Publication Data
Sullivan, Rosemary
The bone ladder

Poems.
ISBN 0-88753-334-5

I. Title.
PS8587.U483B65 2000   C811'.54   C00-900316-9
PR9199.3.S856B65 2000

Cover: Photogaph of my grandfather Jeremiah Guthrie with his bicycle
(1895). According to Aunt Mary, he had just won the track record for the
fastest cyclist in North America: one mile in one minute, twenty-three
seconds.

Cover design by John Doherty.

for
Danny, Laurie, Christopher,
Tara, Gavin and Keenan

Table of Contents

FROM: *LIFE SENTENCE: A CHILEAN SEQUENCE*

GRANADA NOTEBOOK

The Space a Name Makes

Sisters

Each summer when the others left for camp
we carted the mattress to the backyard
to build our tent – an eerie laundry
hanging in moonlight.

I was thirteen months behind you,
watching from a distance the body
you ran to meet so suddenly
those nights we lay in cooling dark

listening to the crickets drumming
the pulse of summer, the moon
an old woman leaning
through cracks in our blanket walls.

Your body was the mystery I waited for
from my childish space, the bones
shifting slowly like some creature
surfacing inside you.

Your breast spots stretching you
out of my world
the night he called to you
took off his clothes carefully

a ritual danced in moonlight,
daring you to come out;
you only laughed
and told me never to tell.

I did, of course, caught off balance
in that zone families clear
for a middle child –
perhaps it was then I cut my face

from all the family photos –
when I look at them now
there is always a small hole
sitting in the corner

I started spelling my name backwards,
retreating from the space a name makes.

Kind with my betrayal,
you understood the child roaming sadly in a body.

The tent gone, another summer;
the creature stretched me too
as I watched night after night
the mirror, alone in my room.

You are still the guide in my dreams
teaching me to leap gaps between spaces,
still the loved one waiting patiently
for the childish dreamer to catch you.

The Green Hat

A punctuation mark, it sits in the middle
of my childhood. It was a telescope –
each green cylinder fitting into the next –
I wore like a third eye
to keep the world at a distance.

First hat – my own. Others had fallen haphazardly
from my mother's fingers (or the aunts
who dropped their Good Will into our lives
and departed).

My Easter resurrection hat
floating above the new coat repeated
three times like a chorus on the shining
bodies of my sisters in the church.

I'd wanted it to be beautiful
but secretly I hated that hat,
kneeling in the Father's house
suffering a world
never large enough
to love him.

In its afterlife the hat still surfaces
an old habit I unravel
thread by thread,
trying to understand how a green hat
can bring all the weight of childhood
back to my head.

Farmer's Daughter

I spent the longest time
trying to find you,
the vague woman in a house
roaring with a man's need.

I searched old photographs –
in your anxious hands,
that nub of womb-fresh life
is me, your face still
farm-fresh, warm as an egg.

The smallest thirteenth child
lost at the back of a family
hating cows.

I remember your mother's house,
the root cellar yawning.
When you ran home that time
she spoke of made beds
and sent you packing.

Life was the threat
you learned from brothers,
hands as big as shovels.
You looked for the strong man
who came from the sky
in a World War II movie
to fold his body over you
like a cape.

It took me years to see
the still-born thing
you had buried.

It surfaced once.

On my marriage night
you broke your code and cried:
"Don't leave me."

I hid those words for years
knowing we too dug hands like shovels
into your life.

Euclid Street

She stands on the porch, late.
The same light she saw as a child
pins the mountain ash
to the grass scattered with berries.
Behind her, the room she was born in
and the one where she hid her body
to protect, like a secret
until she could get it safely away.

There were always too many lives in other rooms –
the anxious man tied to a job for fifty years
till the company paid him off
with a piece of the building mounted
on a bronze plaque. He needed to drink
to see the joke. And the timid woman
who filled the house with her bright red heart
asking for nothing except a life.

When they fought she would cower
in the shrinking corners with her three sisters,
each one planning escape into the arms of someone
they would also have to abandon.
Love is like that. It's the need
you run from and return to
always circling back to where you started
like somebody lost.

The houses retreat behind doors and the racoons
begin their scuttle across the tired lawns,
stopping to drink from the sprinklers
spreading a thin rain against the drought.
She remembers the street the child lived on –
a snow-tunnel, its ten-foot drifts pocked with holes
she hid inside and watched –
the street edged with the ditch that swelled
to a sucking mouth in the spring
and took her down once
into its belly.

Behind the doors other lives taunted
with their order on loan from Eaton's,
their sleek, stubborn brightness

15

colluded in, like guilt.
Mr. Goodman drank himself to death when the kids left
and Mrs. Adams finally cleaned herself into a corner
of the livingroom you couldn't enter with shoes.

Each family carries its load of ordinary pain.
She's taken ten years
to know this, standing on a porch thinking
of the slow decantation of lives
and she can't put together its meaning.

Childhood

All day I would wait for the sun
to fall like a cold thought,
then race through the stand of trees
lost at the bottom of the garden
hunting the fear –
Running till I reached the swamp
where wild calla cowered
beneath white hoods
and bullheads thrust up fists.
When I'd circled the tree
I could go back –
Night after night the escape,
the hand on the handle as I pushed the bolt,
the terror sweet as a drug
feeding the need.

Rest Home: Hay Bay

For me she was always
Aunt Mary down on the farm
where I watched the turtles
lug themselves from the pond
big as garden tables
lumbering over the fields
each failing summer.
" They last a hundred years,"
Uncle Nellis said,
his cane beating their backs
till they lunged, snapping
at air. All afternoon
leaping the sea-high hay
our bodies supple waves,
scaring the cows. " Hoodlums,"
Mary laughs, holding
the day in broken hands.

They've put you out to rest,
the little that's left –
your body sinking beneath
humped shell, the stubbled
stranger's face, mouth lipless
biting last bits of life,
only the eyes still quick,
their shrewd sidling attack.

Old turtle, I loved your book,
the sepia photos curled
with the years you've storied.
Grandpa Guthrie leans on the bike
he rode for Canada the day
he fell. " The Americans bribed
the water-boys." He died
ten years later. And Aunt Rose
with her circus man,
her parents' warning:
"Entertainers drift."
When she turned him down,
he poisoned the tea. She was
simple Aunt Rose after that.

All our stories saved
in your careful schoolmarm script.

Now words betray you,
not to be found.
I cannot bear the hurt
shake of your head,
the notebook with only your name
repeated neatly in columns
like a child learning
its first lesson.

In your tired shoes you say
won't need replacing
clutching your empty book,
you can't believe that
life can take so much
and still be life.
It's not the dying.
Rather the terrible watching
the mind's dissolve,
you helpless, a turtle
flung on its back,
and worse, the body sits on
in a room after you've gone
rotting like any shell.

Lake Atitlan

The flutist sits on a bamboo pier in my mind
knees carefully crossed, back straight
facing the water
and suddenly the image moves with the memory
of his playing
notes ride out across clear water slicing the mists
and scaling the blue volcanoes
until all is a rich blue harmony
of sound held like a glass globe
on a recessed shelf of my mind
from where I take it
and play it
like a flutist on a bamboo pier

One More Human Thing

Ruins always move us
more than standing structures;
it is the poignancy
of one more human thing lost.

How beautiful this naked stone
stripped and exposed;
domes like mouths open to sky;
archways holding up air;
cracks snaking their surface
with rumours of final disintegration.

At the Convent of the Capuchinas
the nuns' cells are the size of graves
and effegies sit in their nuns' garb
praying behind skulls of death.
I listen to dogs barking in the distance,
smells of cooking rising from the town.
Sweet voices echo in the tower of retreat like bells
and the nuns are here.

Their laughter rings
over the brilliant tiles in the sun.
They gather flowers in the garden
from the zapotes for their altars.
In the hallways they scurry to supper
over each other's heels.
One sits in her cell where doors never close,
gazes at blue volcanoes and longs for home.

The town didn't want them –
young girls taken from poverty to serve God
on the backs of the poor.
Their peace lasted thirty years
till the earthquake brought them down
and the death they had been searching for
came to them, no more welcome
in this disguise than any other.

Hunting for Tropical Plants in the Golfo

Dawn shakes the trees awake
and reddens the river to attention
between ink-blue mountains
emitting their darkness like smoke.

We set off in the quiet waters,
hats in our hands, listening
to the wind advancing down the lake,
buffing the water to a soft skin
for the pelicans to scavenge.
Rio Dulce – sweet river smelling of watermelons.

The jungle is alive with light,
ramon trees turn hands as we pass,
palmleaved pinwheels spin.
The lianas are deadly fer-de lance
webbing a dark warning.

All day we hunted bromelias,
gaudy pink parasites
that lit the jungle with flares.
We climbed for hours
ripping bromelias from branches.

Flaming suns plunged to our boats
and we were a cargo of flowers
lacing through green waters,
the suns breaking
about our burning shoulders.

Market Day

The smell of a green world breaks through the dust.
I stand on a rim of suction,
colours pull me in:
crimson pomegranates and cool yellow grenadillos,
greem lucma, pale white toronja, pumpkin and quince.
They ring bells against my eyes.
Women in hooped skirts and black stovepipe hats,
children in bright rebozos staring from their backs.
A ragged girl, peacock bright, offers me a pineapple:
"Oje gringa – mucho dinero," she smiles slyly.
Four bluebirds flutter in her net.
She would have me take them to my country.
The mangoes and melons and papayas call out in sweetness
fruits of water in a dry world;
above the market, mud houses gleam in tiers.

Temple of the Double-Headed Serpent: Tikal

Anthropologists conjecture that the
high priest was born on the temple and
never descended

I was born on this lip of stone
jutting out over the jungle.
I've never wanted to go down.
As a child I would run to the edge to catch the birds
or follow the lizards with my hand along the ledges
and I wondered what earth was like underfoot
it's so cool and soft in the fingers.
Now I sit and watch my world.
The trees sway like swarms of settled birds
and the sounds drift up to me of the monkey's frenzy.
At dawn I watch the fresh god break through the tired mouth of earth
and I draw him up with my will.
I am other now
my back as hard as this stone
my eye on everything that moves.

The Sad Story of Doña Beatriz de la Cueva

Don Pedro died when a horse fell on him in the town of Nocheztlan.
When they asked where the pain was he said: In my soul.
His grief-stricken widow Doña Beatriz had the palace painted with black clay
and all the furniture blacked for nine days of mourning.
The court plotted Doña Beatriz's murder
but she countered by having all the conspirators arrested.
On the final day of mourning she appointed herself La Sin Ventura
the first governess in the Americas.
The peasants were shocked, then frightened when the rains started
and day by day the water fell in sheets.
Lightning lashed the city with all the powers of the heavens.
At midnight on the tenth day the earth heaved.
Agua coughed and sent his mud rolling into the city.
In the black coffin palace the unlucky one
flew to the chapel with her daughter and eleven maidservants
but her forty hour reign was ended.
The flood and shifting earth brought the battered palace down
around the ears of Doña Beatriz
that women should know God did not mean the city to be ruled by females.

Woman on Bloor Street

She surfaces at intervals –
always unexpected –
emptied on a street corner
rapt by the waste of sky
or poking a finger
among desolate vegetables
staring from their sidewalk bins.

In summer she wears a grey wool coat,
the fox collar from Honest Ed's
turned up against the sun.
Beneath her pink straw hat –
the brim slides provocatively in your direction –
her body suddenly melts.
She's round like one of those punch dolls
in the nursery. She pops back.

The pills have melted her,
and the endless fumblings of interns
fingering her brain for holes.
But her face is the face of a young woman
beautifully painted and hidden beneath her hat;
occasionally she offers it to you
like a present –
so shy –
It's the only thing she's saved.

The Fugitive Heart

Today he brought his heart to us in a black bag.
It looked like an ocharina huddled beside the silver flute,
a fat orange bulb with holes to blow on.
He slipped it out when we weren't looking
and it sat in the corner watching us.

It was wary, his orphan heart, careful of exits,
dreaming of women and kisses.
It wrapped itself around the table leg
and talked of life under bridges
where stray children fucked dogs for food.
A hungry heart with knives in its fingers,
scouring the streets for women to sell.

When you kill and you hear the soft hiss
of life leak from a body,
the heart looks itself in the face.
It sees only a fat sponge
that sucks the air with blood.
"So that's life," he said.

I watched his eyes retreat to the back of his face;
the heart on the table now,
a taut grey sack.
He picked it up delicately
like a blister
and put it back inside his coat.

An Argentinian Script

for Nestor Fantini

You speak of one afternoon –
the sun was doing its yellow dance
across the café table.
Above the rim of your cup
a car stopped. Two men
descended a street
as in a film –
where the extras go on with their business
pretending not to notice
and the street is just a pretext
to pull the plot together –
suddenly you knew the script

All your life
you've dragged these men
behind you.

This is the moment
you dream each night, differently.
But always the same wall,
the same hot hiss of lead,
waking, when the blindfold's off,
among the dead
and the ones whose hair turned white,
five times, five deaths,
undied,
screaming inside your head.

Tree Man

for Juan

The morning traffic begins its slow shuffle
through the city.
Don Manuel slips past our garden gate
on his way to the factory.
He is happy: Our bright red tomatoes
leap into sun.
We've been awake all night.

I have come from another country,
one you made for me
with words. It was dusk there
but the sky gathered its colours
for a final fling
and the birds sucked
the last flecks of light from the shadows.

I watched you.
You leaned against a tree
and the tree leaned back.
I cannot explain except that you changed skins –
Your eyes grew green and vegetal
and the tree breathed in you,
blooding your breath with leaves.

When you hold me now
I taste earth in your mouth,
am loved as a tree loves,
with all its roots and branches.

Man After My Own Heart

I could wear your body
like you wear my jeans –
It's a mirror fit.
Already we get mixed up.

Those nights careening
from the edge of flesh –
your sex my root.
We could switch.

When melt-down comes:
you/me   I/you
split to a new space;
my heart swinging
in your ribs.

Wanted

It was your hands –
those roots. They broke
my dream one night
rising, like Arthur's sword
out of the lake.
Just your kind of joke.

What I loved then
was to see you naked,
the proud, self-mocking way
you strutted –
flying your sex
over my water bed.

In that crazy room
with the glow-tape stars
you were intrepid,
rushing in on every side
till I rose and wanted
you staring with your green eyes
through my green eyes.

Telluric Man

for Gustavo Estrada

Hands full of earth
you came to me and said:
"Here – make me a path."
We walked for hours.
Space stretched out. No sound –
only our feet on blistered leaves.
We entered a clearing
closed by a circle of trees.
The sky gone.
You knelt
and listened to the sound of roots,
the dark telluric sound
groaning downwards.
You scraped at the soil like a dog.
In the blackness
I saw the trees
clutching the shadows of rock,
the grotesque shapes they assumed
pared to that desperate longing.
In a rage you tore at the ground.
Hairy roots bled earth in your hands.
Suddenly your body stiffened,
the sounds of human sobbing.
You covered them over with soil.
There was nothing to do but go back.

The Reaching

In all those years
I never noticed your hands
frail at the end of your body,
looming like a noise to distract them.

They are afraid of the fatally human
and hide behind pale nails like closed eyelids.

You talk of the problems of a desire
that pulls the body where it doesn't want to go.

You tell your hands to stop you
but they have turned to soft thoughts
and betray you with reachings.

At this moment they reach for me,
shamefaced, curling with questions,
falling liquid into my hands.

Aristophanes' Hermaphrodite

People are sentimental.
They love a love story.
Imagine an egg – four arms, four legs, two heads
twisting like periscopes on a tubular neck,
the globular man/woman sitting plaintively
in the backs of our imaginations.
He said it was sliced like an apple
for pickling and now the pieces go skulking
for each other in the dark.
But love is an old story we all edit.
Imagine the fights
in the great domestic egg.
Would one side or back
(but what is back and front?)
be stronger? When it wanted to go
forward (but what is forward?)
would it hoist the other legs on its back
and tramp off on its own private journeys?

Is that why men dream
of hoisting women in the air and walking
off into sunsets? – perhaps it's an old dream.
Would the front half do all the talking
while the back loomed like a shadow
always excluded from conversations,
the half everybody took for granted
and no one remembered
peeking over a shoulder to slip a word in?
Would they search each other's bodies
like Braille, four hands groping in the night?
Asleep in bed on their sides
in the terrible obscurity of their intimacy
would they dream the utopian dream
of separation?
Ideal love is an old joke
people keep missing. It's harder than that,
to keep the seal intact and meet the other
front-on – face to lonely face.

Love Story: The Colin Thatcher Murder Trial

Prologue

The story told below is invented
from facts. Lives loom
behind facts, slipping loose –
a man, two women,
a child.
We're never what we seem
but what we need.
This is an allegory of fracture,
of life as it turns away
on a course set centuries back.
The point of the story is to change it.

His Story

Each year I visit my father's grave.
I loved him. A hard man, my father,
but he lived. His way.
A man has to hold his life together
starting with nothing. Have you stood alone
on prairie in the winter,
you the only thing standing
for miles? It wipes you out –
that white, unless you fight it.
When I was young I hated him
out on the farm. He used to bait me.
He laughed when the hands
tried to drown me in the lake.
They almost did, I was that useless.
Once I cut the balls off his prize bull;
if he'd caught me he'd have killed me.
Those years I learned –
working a bullwhip into a post.
You can still see where I wore
the wood down with my lashings.
You have to shape the world to what you want.
My father made mistakes.
He needed love. He didn't trust us.
He didn't want me in politics –

thought people might use me to get him.
He died two months after the election.
They rode him out. They always do.
My mother understood him.
Sure, she catered, wouldn't smoke
in front of him. He thought it loose,
but she was always loyal
the way a woman should be.
It's in the word. The woman for the man.
He made us, with the ranch
and the apartments and the cars.
She kept the house together –
big dinners at Christmas with the family.
She gave me my first gun
for hunting, knew I had it
in me. She was always there
waiting for trophies I brought her.
When I married I thought that was it.
At first it was. I met her by fluke on a date –
thought I was getting another woman
but she was lovely, shy and gentle,
a scared filly. She was fresh.
Never had a man before me. I pinned her
and we dated. The honeymoon was hard.
Mostly I remember
I burned the soles of my feet
lying on the sundeck – harder walking
but it got good. Seventeen years of good
till she turned. She got ideas
from the courses she was taking.
I should have known. She decorated
my best friend's office and screwed him.
The bitch. We fought.
Sure, I'd got a little wild –
too much money. Silk corduroy suits
and women. Late home some nights –
her crying. When she fell from the ladder
and caught my elbow, she said I hit her.
But I didn't. I loved her.
When she left I couldn't eat,
sleep, worse than the death
of a child. I begged her to come back.
Men are weak on sex. When you have power
women stick like flies to flypaper.
She knew that, knew I was wild.

I used to call the cops from my ranch
and tell them I was leaving. They'd catch me
doing a-hundred-and-twenty down the freeway.
I kept those guys in Chivas.
When she went for the kids and the money –
that's when I had to stop her.
Did she think I'd give her the girl
to bring up in the gutter?
Yes, I thought of killing her.
My fuse is short. She was bleeding me.
A bullet costs only a dollar,
but I'm not crazy. She turned
the courts against me. The kids
saw through her. My son knew
she gave me the clap once,
knew what a whore was. I was at home
with them when it happened.
Only a monster would kill a woman.
I'm not a monster.
Ask the guard. I arranged for him
to take my little girl with his kid
trick-or-treating. It's always
the little ones who suffer.
She'll be thirty when she sees me out.
I thought I'd win this one –
even had the tickets for Florida.
The bitch got me. It was in the cards.
I haven't given up. In jail
I get religion. I read
from the bible. I sit alone
in my cell, empty.
Something collapses inside
like when a foot sinks into mud
you think will hold it.
The light falls through the window
on the page and it happens.
I feel my father's hand
lifting mine a way I don't remember.
It was so large. I somehow feel
his comfort. Born again. Telling me
a strong man can never be broken.

The Mistress

I have to admit it's a strange feeling
to blow your wife away,
he said and kind of smiled.
The words hooked me – they reeled me in.
Something in a woman loves a murderer.
Sex is the bargain
we always arrange to lose.

He plotted the murder for years
out in the desert with a hand gun
snapping necks off empty Perrier bottles.
Each one was human.
He was back before dark
for a round of golf with his kids.

I was the witness listening
for coded messages from the long-distance
absence where he lived.
"I'm going out now," he'd say.
This may be the night. Stick around
before he slipped on his orange wig
and slid behind the Olds
to cruise the streets.
Once he shot through the window.
He laughed after.
Hadn't gauged the thickness of the glass;
the bullet a slain thing in snow.
The police forgot to check him,
forgot that a man always wants to kill his wife.

I laughed with him.
The sex was good that night.
He was charming.
And deadly.
I'd learned the art of those moods.
Sex is death;
the hot sticky sinking that makes and breaks you.
Loved like death.
I watched the bruises swell on the face
that wasn't my face
but a child's cowering in a corner
waiting for the rip of love.

In that violence at least
I knew I was owned.

I tried to kill myself once with 292s
but that was silly.
He reminded me of the rules:
I was the weak one.
If I left I would die more quickly
than if I stayed.
Things made sense that way.
He was the man in the silk suit
who came first-class.
He'd crawled into my body
looking for his life.
If he lashed out like a wounded thing,
he was the hurt one everyone failed.
Maybe I could save him
staring out at the world
across his need.
But my body was useless.
Inside something sad was loose.
It listened and feared and thought
but was never enough.
It was ashamed to show itself.
It deserved to die.

Then I saw the woman's picture in the newspaper.
He'd held her like a dog by the collar
and slashed her face.
Her broken wrist and hand
twisted at her side.
I was outraged.
Death should be clean not vulgar,
the necessary death
of love.

When I called the police
I said: I never lied
I just did nothing.
Anyway, he wasn't the kind of man
worth dying for.

A Child is Alone

In the photographs the reporters took
the others have closed their eyes;
only hers are open, stare into blankness.
She's inside her head rehearsing
the day her mother came to get her,
the day she watched her brother
punch her mother in the face,
screaming, "You bitch."
She'd heard her father use that word.
Mothers were bitches when they left
and you hit them.
If only they'd stop flashing lights in her face.
("You're daddy's an important man," grandma said.
People want to see us.")
But she mustn't speak to them.
"We have to be here for daddy. He needs us."
They were walking through deep snow
making empty holes with their feet.
She couldn't feel her body
hidden inside the cape she wore
so people wouldn't see her.
They are going to the big building
they call the court. She wonders
if her father lives there.
He hasn't been home six months,
since the day the policemen
stopped the car and took him.
She sits in the front with grandma
and the man who talks for her father.
Her brother is there too.
He squeezes her hand when they bring him out
and put him in the box.
He looks so big. His face is angry
till he sees her and the smile cracks it.
She wonders what she did.
When he put her on the horse at the ranch
and told her to be brave
she knew she mustn't show the fear
that sat in her throat.
She tried to keep her mouth closed and swallow.
It wouldn't stay inside and she cried.
Daddy expected you to please him

but her mother was too sad,
especially after those nights
she heard them fighting in their room
and had to hide under the pillow
to stop the noise.
Daddy used that word then
and her mother's face was hurt
where she fell out of the bed.
Something between her parents.
She thought it might involve the man
they called her uncle.
It upset her.
That's when her mother left.
Her father said she only wanted money now
for the new man she lived with
and loved better than us.
She tried to comfort him.
She combed his hair at night in the big chair –
it had a thick oily smell in her fingers.
But he was angry and went away mostly.
Sometimes alone in bed
her mouth felt strange.
Her tongue was a block of fuzz growing
and she was worried for her face.
She knew it was empty and someone might erase it.
Her mother was dead now.
She's afraid of what God could do
because of what daddy called her.
In school they said God has no body.
It was hard to image where he would be.
When they showed the pictures in the court
she knew her daddy didn't do it.
She didn't see the pictures
but she heard the man describe them,
the man grandma said only told lies.
She leaned over and asked,
"Are we going to win this one?"
They only smiled and didn't answer.
She tries to lose herself in the story she's reading.
Nancy Drew is searching for the mystery of the locket –
The thief left it in her room
and she knows by the picture inside
someone is in danger.
She has to save someone.
When her father and brother refused

to go to the funeral she went alone.
The smells of the flowers made her dizzy
but the songs echoing on the high ceiling helped
and she watched the candle stubs flicker,
each one an angel guarding her mother
in the black box studded with flowers.
She knew she would never see her mother again.
Tomorrow they will say the verdict.
"Daddy's going to have a party," grandma said.
Tomorrow it will be all right again.

Letter to My Daughter

Last night I dreamt a funeral.
Mine. Only you were there.
Your upturned innocent face.
My hand flung out;
your touch broken.
Such a bitter parting.
I fear for my life now;
I must find words to help you.

You are too young to know
the chilled spaces
a man and woman can live in.
I loved your father
at first
but the damage was so far back –
not to be dug out –
a man falling
into the hole of himself.

He flailed
when the world shifted an inch
from his grasp,
when I shifted, needing myself.

He hid behind his mask
and never saw its fasteners.
The world permits that
in a man. I saw the child
looking through clouded pupils.

We are all hurt
but some of us kill.
I can't explain this.

I don't say easily I forgive him
or the world –
Could I have fled my life?
I needed you.
You are in danger.

I watched you walking in woods
behind the house so desolate,

turning the bruised leaves up.
My heart in my throat.
You came innocent
not knowing what you entered.

I lost your brother;
I can't bear to lose you.
Don't trust him.
I always knew the rage
loose in the house
would yield to this conclusion.
There is nothing now to stop him.
I know it hurts. I'm sorry.
We are hand-in-hand in terror.
You must save yourself
for me. I love you.
Will you understand this?

Etcetera

Sometimes the monster in us erupts.
We line up by the hundreds
in winter blizzards to cadge a seat.
We read the papers faithfully,
fascinated when the brain cells go rioting
and the masks fall at our feet.
We take sides looking for the motive
pieced together by reporters,
relieved when somebody gets it.
We long for the catharsis
that will keep this at a distance –
but for the grace of God etcetera.
It's time to remember, being human,
we invent all stories.
It happened centuries back:
a man and a woman alone and together.
We've got to change the rules.

FROM:

BLUE PANIC

Words

Aunt Mary used to warn me about words.
They never stay where you put them.
They're loose.
Any no-good can use them.
Like a woman, she tried
to keep them safe in the family.

Family was her story that added down to me
– always fenced with a lesson:
Words break loose if you let them.

She stored the family photos in a basket.
Trussed up in her rocker, warty as any gourd,
each night her hands plunged the corridors of blood.
I knew she was hooked on danger.

She could go all the way back to wind,
how it falls and picks itself up in a field.
Or fog empties a valley till all you see
is your hands where the world was.

From her I learned there were others
pacing inside me.
She said they had made me up.
I was meant to love them.

But it terrified me to think I was lived in
by strangers I had never met
or knew only by name.
They made me alien fiction.

In my bones
an old woman dies over and over.
I dare not look
in the room with the blooded axe
nor speak to the men who walked out.
Their tracks in my blood. Their lust
for edges.

I could spend
a lifetime digging graves
in my head.

Return Journey

Swerving West, the snow threaded us
a cat's cradle. We hung for a moment
in its fingers. I watched
the wind take over, suck us
into the white smother.

Hours it seemed we drove down pulleys of light.
No sound, only a heavy breathing
ours and the wind's.

As if the world were nothing,
as if we'd swerved
into the white throat
of night.

Suddenly red flared in the distance,
the skeleton of a house
burning against the ice
calling us back to our fear.

Elegy

for D.P.

A man, thirty-three, in an olive-green coat,
singing: "Looking for My Shanghai Lil" with a smile
sitting on the edge of his face,
barely –
That's how I remember you
across a café in Paris
watching the door.
Not young. Easy to open.
Valises comparing our wares.

In the safe space under the city's rafters
you'd cleared and hung with fragile
wooden birds gathered in Finland,
we drank good wine and thought
of ourselves as survivors.
You tended me like a wound
feeding me oeufs anglais and espresso
before disappearing into the underground
with the rest of the morning.
At night your mouth pushed hungrily into mine,
the kind of hurt I loved then,
an echo in a man.

In her note she'd left kisses all over your body.
She was dying slowly in another country,
the disease that turns the body
too sweet to hold.
Strange that you could neither go nor stay.
Easier to die your own death
than live another's.
In the sweat of August in that small room
you drew an X over the door
and left your name behind you.

Here is another letter,
long past sending, to say
people can open briefly
like the circle you clear on a winter window
with warm breath.

You feel a loss
incommensurate with your own wanting,
for the way lives have of eluding each other
and going missing.

Sisters of the Holy Name

We were their daughters,
those faithful nuns,
married to Christ,
the gold band they'd lain down for
gleaming on firm fingers
as we filed past in pencil rows
each morning.

Those were the days God woke me,
a dependable alarm, and I watched him
rise from clouds on the church wall,
the incense sharp in our nostrils
high on the Latin Litany.

How many persons are there in God?
the priest asked as the nuns fussed
in their starched habits
calling him father.
We could smell the wine on his breath
that rasped behind the grille
we dragged our sins to each week.

Clean like fresh laundry,
I wanted to die
and go to heaven directly.
Already afraid to touch that place
between my legs where the devil lived,
a mole in a wet nest.
When I looked with a mirror
I could almost see his red face.

The Table

Nobody planned this
table stretching its broad grin
across the floor, loaded with lives.

It's the house. Some nights
it wants. We come,
pulled by a stronger will,
unwittingly, to family
its geography of need.

Santiago's in the kitchen
hacking thin potato slivers
crisp, ambiguous as memories,
placed like wafers on our plates.
They are an augury. We squirm,
a thin laughter rises in the heat.

Adriana watches the lampshade
swing a hex across the ceiling.
She tells us how one night
she tied her husband to his bed,
eyes propped open with toothpicks,
while she took another man.
It was revenge he had to see.

Her son Sergito guards the door.
His father's disappeared.
In his tiny mind the memory climbs.
He beats a drum in anger,
takes pennies from a jar,
holds them over open palms,
a practised ritual, pulling back
before the pennies drop. He knows
already to withhold.

Ricardo plays the guru of the kitchen.
If you paint a balloon with dots
collapse it to one point,
that's space and time. The centre
nowhere. Everywhere the centre.
The universe contracted to a table.

We play at the illusion
of a moment. The house
erupts:
oasis in our scattering.

The Poem Fights With the Buzz-Saw

The buzz of Don Manuel's saw
blurts from the back of his garden.
He is making something again,
but the poem can't get itself written.
The words buckle under the racket
searching for a man who left
his country to build a fence
around ten square feet of earth.

He lives in his garden here.
It's safer than a house.
Too many thoughts rattle around in rooms.
Outside at the back where he grows things
tomatoes climb in their cages,
mint crawls under the fence
confusing the late smells of summer.
Already the grapes are purpling on the arbour.
But teeth keep biting deeper into wood
and the sound whines over the pink morning.
The sun sits in the trees
watching from a slight distance.

When I told Don Manuel our wall
collapsed in the kitchen
carrying so many pieces of our history
he only smiled and said: *You must always be ready
to build another wall.*

I met his wife on the subway.
She doesn't speak the tongue here
and cleans the insides of other houses.
When I mentioned going back to his country
he said: *It's hard to leave a garden.*
Only the son lives in the house.
He is young and Canadian now
and remembers less.

LIFE SENTENCE: A CHILEAN SEQUENCE

Exile

One day a life stopped.
Was that It?
Shelved? Suspended on a hook?

A man packed a country
in a suitcase with his shoes
and left.

Travelling
the spaces in between –
the not-here   the not-there:

what you had been
now sealed
in someone else's story.

The dead end
with no return ticket

except in your head
so that nowhere
was quite real

and the sentence for life:
to look back.

Passe-Port

We pass the turnstile
into your country.
The computer spits you out –
You're no longer on its mind.

I always thought a country
was the way the trees unleave
in your head or the snow
falls on your childhood, thought it
part of the landscape you become.
The stories that sink roots into history
and repeat themselves like litanies:
the family,
bone-ladder you descended
from somewhere.

But you tell me a country
is really a door.
They can close it.

Talca: City of Thunder

This could be my town,
the one I always wanted to leave.
The houses lean diffident and anxious
along mainstreet, suspects in a lineup.
The lights keep the street on a tight rein.

There's the drugstore,
the cheap shoeshop,
the oculist a cut above the rest.
There's the store with pretensions to fashion.
Wild-haired mannequins parade in its eyes.

The jakarinds crowd the cupola
in the town square where old men play chess.
The cathedral points a bone at the sky.

I feel I've lived on your street
in these houses of no face;
windows shuttered, turned inward,
hearts a sealed garden
spreading lives, rooms, roots.

They are relentlessly female, make
family weather: Square sun
to a private courtyard,
filter rain to a need.

Outside your house there's the tree
you shimmied down naked
nights your mother stole your clothes.
She thought to keep you in.
But the point of a wall
is to climb it; of a street,
to take it. And a town like this?
To leave it.

Like family,
it always pulls you back.

The Plastic Landscape

This is an ordinary street.

We slip home drunk at 4:00 A.M.
when the café closes.
The sentry with the machine gun
looks plastic in his box.
He's part of the landscape.
I can't hear the ghosts
of the ones tortured
in the mayor's office.

You were jailed at the bottom
of this street – something about a play.
You were Oedipus. When the crunch came
you gouged your eyes out.
They were offended by so much blood.
They were always more discrete.

Her House

It is her last gamble,
this house where she waits all day
for endings. She never moves,
a small grey rock barnacled
for eighty years with lives.
She is idea now. Her will
surveys the scattered bones
of her intent.
No one enters.

Behind, her house stretches
its secret body.
It is filled with left over women,
emptied with children.
All day flowers drop from their fingers.
They sell them in the market.
The meals repeat themselves
like hunger.

From her counter she watches
bodies pass into shadow.
The street dead-ends at the prison
where her son was tortured.
She never turns her mind
in that direction.
The world is this door
narrowed to a tolerable slice.

Bringing Home the Tree

In the park the magnolia explode
like Christmas crackers
pretending to be snow.
The children carry bright wishes
to Santa sweating in his red suit.
I'm laughing because Joseph's pacing
in his manger.

We're bringing home the tree.
Ten feet shuffling beneath green fir,
a centipede pacing the streets
of the city of thunder.

Claudia in the lead,
slipping off the cliff of adolescence,
star on our top-most branch.
Then Margarita, little girl-man
in her pinned-up jeans.
And La Paz, our furtive bird peering
for a moment from her dark cover.

They're shouting at the tops of their voices
Tio Chiche! Tio Chiche!
Uncle "little-rattle in the baby carriage."
They're leading you home.

You're the clown they've waited for.
You're their best game.

Christmas in the Barrios

In the newspaper this morning
the headlines promise
PRESENTS WILL DROP FROM THE SKY.
The soldiers will deliver our Christmas gifts
from their helicopters.
We've told the children to be ready
for dolls to drop in our streets,
skirts flying, swinging their legs.
If some come in pieces, an eye here,
a leg there, not to cry.
We can fix them
in the toy hospital.

Panzer-man will land with his tin sword
on our rooftops; houses with their tea sets
fall in our gardens; puzzles
rain on our doors.

Some people are afraid
but I tell them it's good training.
In Chile
laughter is black.
It always falls
on our head.

Santiago

Once this was your theatre –
Acting classes ended at the Café Cerro
where the drama began. Like the night
they sat the cadaver at the table
drinking toasts till dawn.
He'd wanted to be here once after he died.
The poets and the pimps competing in women
and stories.

Now the streets are actors,
made up, and the people we meet
pretend they know you. Nobody's changed
though dead years float
in gutters under their eyes.

You can see only the bones of buildings,
the street beneath the street,
the negative before it was fixed
in time's solution.
You are a tourist in your own present
in a city you wanted to be in
once
after you died.

Memorias

You test a street before you take it.
This one percolates fear.
Outside the riot squad picks up the night's stragglers.

Till dawn we've eaten *chancho en piedra*
scooping hands into the stone crock
like a baptism.
They bring us books that don't exist here.
Undercover agents on somebody's hit list.

They tell me they can feel the holes in their heads
where people disappeared,
how they troll in twilight spaces
bringing up the odd shoe.

I'm learning freedom isn't the moon.
Someone else can own it.

The Necessary Paranoia

Life shows its stiff upper lip.
It never breaks old habits.
This is Christmas. We shop.
There are seventeen presents to buy.
We think each gift through.
We do this for hours.

Till dark. On a night pass
we visit the other country:
There's something you have brought.

We are laughing and trading lives
when you ask it:
Do you know who we are? Can you trust us?

This is your gift:
You must learn the necessary paranoia.
Mistrust is the pride you have left.
Carry it in your skin like chameleons.
Watch yourself disappear down a street.
Freedom is the bitter crevice,
the fault line just at your feet.

The Thief

Our bus careens over the backs of cars,
belches its innards. This is rush hour
any time of day. The rush is to sell.
Each furtive stop someone leaps up –
six Band-Aids, a safety belt,
ice trays offered in ransom
to the heat. A basket
comes down the aisle on legs.

At Alemeda we pick up an old man
in a T-shirt. He lurches in his bones
like a passenger, the smile sliding
off the side of his face.
He begs for our ears like Antony.

Citizens, I'm a thief, he says.
Freedom is hunger. At least in jail
we ate. I don't want to steal you purses.
Help me rehabilitate.
In our country
only the big thief eats.

We grin. The pesos drop
into his hat.

It's Almost Over

I met a man here
who walks to death like an office.
Every day. He does not call this
courage. Fear is his habit.
He walks it casually.

He tells me there's a trick about fear.

At first you think you're a room,
locked and creaky. You dare not look
through the keyhole. At the door of yourself
you keep your silent vigil.
After years you get lonely.
One day you open the door.
The fear is pacing inside you.
You see it is human. It has your face.
You pick it up and walk it into sunlight.
You're no longer alone.
There are thousands on this street.

Elegy for Pablo Neruda

We have driven to Isla Negra
looking for Neruda. His house
is sealed by order of the state.
The woman who tends the garden
calls through a crack in the gate: *Prohibido.*

We measure his steps to the beach:
each paling of the fence signed by a witness.
The rocks are painted with his face,
a stone fist breaks the naked skyline.

He broods the tombed vision: The palace bombed;
his friend dead; twelve brief days
to write this down and follow his grief
to its deadly conclusion.

In the distance the lights of Veña
cross-hatch to a phantom net
still marking the wreckage.
The raging surf interrogates the sand,
the mountains throw back his words
blade-narrow: *Yo Acuso.*

Seascape

I'm at home here on the edge
of a continent. I've seen this before,
the way a beach eases itself into sea.
There's always a last stutter of rocks,
a mist heavy with its stayed breathing
absolving something,
the sun oblique over mountains leaking
their shadows. Skyline of stone.

A man moves bareback on a white horse
over the gull-pocked sand
staring at the sea's neutral distance,

thinking: Unfenced existence,
the curve into heart's dead end,
the loaded secret in the sea's empty blue eye.

Endings

We walk into evening, the last
in your country for the time
being. This is your city as it wants to be.
Lovers in the parks stagger under
the wonder of bodies; the magnolia smell
of laughter and trees flashing arteries
of coloured light. The *empanadas*
steam in their crocks, the musicians
play to our secret wishes,
the vendors pack their leftovers and head home.

We are happy in each other's hands.
I will leave you here and
head to your future. I'm the
homecoming in the epic they've written
you into. To reach me
you must cross these lacunae
alone.

GRANADA NOTEBOOK

Granada Notebook

1.

We left at midnight.
One minute the world emptied, the next,
we were running for our lives.

Down the highway, dead-center
in the windshield — the new moon.
So startling the way it hung beneath the stars.
Orange fin shredding the black wake.

You said: *Like kids running away*
to join the circus.
Can love come down to this?

We slept on the empty beach.
The lake, salt-free, sea-sized, so
beautiful. To stand in the wind
cleansed by the bright light of stars.

2.

You hunting God those nights
naked and mad under the Dagmar streetlights.
God doesn't die, I said, *but it's better
to leave him to his own devices.*
Love, now that's another matter.
Soothing the rain,
as it limps to its own extinction.
I've crawled to my bed at mid-day
exhausting myself, like rain.
Limping to the end of what I took
to be love. And I see it was,
as I untie the intricate fibers
of the heart. Pain, I tell myself,
is only a storm carrying away dead leaves.

3.

Funny how my body always knew first
and my mind only caught on after.
Alone in the house tidying objects.
With the mirror in place and
the pictures straight, I knew
you were lying.

When you walked in the door,
I walked out.
Like a bad film.
Me sitting high in the bus
crossing Dundas, you at the stoplight
in the car passing, blinded,
below. *They missed each other by seconds.*
Whatever lesson we were learning
we kept missing all that bloody summer.

4.

She walked into our lives like she invented us.
Sniffed us out for the dream she needed.
We all needed. What's called love
is ravenous
trailing its beautiful death.
When was it you told me?
And I thought:
Once I loved. Now, I don't.
It seemed simple.
Till you stood before the mirror
and shaved your head.
Those tiny slices in the flesh.
So mad I loved you. That
you could go so far down
till it bled.

5.

The way, in a rainstorm, the sky
descends in sudden violence,
flooding the sluices of the overhead passes
and tumbling to the road in falls
of water, and we wait at the side of the road
filling the space with the hot breath
of our panic, until the violence
has passed and we can proceed
in the dark, the tears of night
blinding our windshield
only a little less.
There has been too much blood
on the walls of my room where I gathered
your body and placed it in the ambulance and you climbed up
whatever fantasy could save you
back into life.
All that still-born anguish.
She tied her bundle quickly and left.
We have all closed doors
on that terrible pain and joined the circus
of the lady contortionist. Runaways,
we pray, day after day,
to the god of lost children,
Save us.

6. GRANADA

A hand rests in the balance
in the Plaza de Alma where the thief swapped it
for two tomatoes. This is a cruel place
of such beauty it batters the heart.
Withered pomegranates still hang
like red fists amid the dead winter foliage.
The white pigeons return to their coop
waiting faithfully the feast of their own death.
I watch the man carry the naked body
of the baby Jesus gingerly by the head.

And you in your bed under feathers
are sleeping off the nightmare.
Can we pick ourselves up like the marionettes
Carlos is making for the fiesta?
Don't look back, he said
or you'll turn to stone.
I would write of love if I could
find the word, love the motive
for all this dying.

7.

Each morning I slip from your skin.
In the museum the dead lie
just as we are lying, folding our bodies
around a question we cannot ask. As if
we are the question we cannot frame.
We had to leave so much behind.
Did it make sense to step out of our lives
leaving them like old clothes on the floor?
They are still there in a heap.
We are running away to the circus,
you shouted over the din of wheels
rolling up the macadam like a black ribbon.
Asleep under the weight of stars.

8.

In the café, floor littered with papers
and discarded cigarettes,
the Virgin sits smiling above the bar.
The gypsy in his blue shirt,
grey hair curled around his chiseled face,
takes a miniature Buddha from his breast pocket,
the one he carries from his second wife.
We are all thieves, he says. *None of us
are princes.* I watch the dogs
come to the same lifting post
outside the window. A child
leans back and licks the rain.
The bells, brassy not beautiful,
hang on the morning.
For the first time I'm at home
in the language.

Today in the Calle Nanque Viejo
a dog gnawing a rat, a ball
of wet matted fur. Head gone.
Rolling in the mouth. I could see the tiny
pink feet between the teeth. He savored it
in front of the Santa Basura.

Here the roosters crow all day. Dissolving time
so you can barely recognize it.

9.

This pit, it magnetizes. Incurving
cliffs sprouting strange weeds,
paddle cacti in the cracks,
its bowl-like bottom full of
tumbled rocks. It is a focus.
Stored in all its hugeness in my mind,
available for troubling dreams.

The valley rolls in great shallow waves.
Everything a buff brown.
Everything dusted over with a fine red silt.
The ground flies up dryly
into my mouth.

10.

In the hills behind our carmen
I walk to the Cross of the Rauda.
It rests above an ancient Arab graveyard.
She was not old, one leg
severed at the knee. Resting the stump,
she laid her crutch across the bench
and what had been her smiling mouth
broke suddenly into a screaming lament
that poured from her tongue
into the ear of the stunted Christ
on his cross. She caressed
his crumpled feet like whipped
disheartened dogs. Like a lover,
touched his carved face of stone.

11.

Here we are, in the city of pomegranates,
the passion fruit that bursts,
leaving its withered shell hanging
like a jagged heart.
Clay brown roofs silvered with weed.
A woman cracks the sky with her red duster.
Down the alleys narrow as blood vessels
sometimes I turn a corner-
and then the mountain's white assault.

The winter light is tender, like the brush
of a cat's back against the leg.
It spills softly into the narrow streets,
half-fills them. Water in a vase.

All is labyrinth and I
am inside the puzzle; there in
the carmen of the Virgin of Angustia,
a sudden stone rose carved in the wall, a garden
of cypress above my head.

Why these tears?
Perhaps only the sheer volume of trumpets and drums
echoing in my chest, or those boys
with their narrow nervous bodies and
cat eyes. Perhaps the simple knowing,
after all this pain,
that I can step into a day
and the day will still be there,
waiting for me.

12.

This is the first snow we've had here.
It started as rain then came down white
to cover our umbrellas.
Poignant somehow to see the spring garden
on the patio fill with snow.
The daisies quiver and frizzle like a girl's hair.
The backless felt seat has a new white cover,
and my wall is punctuated with a long
exclamation of snow.

13.

A small black tornado,
comical, like a coal dust funnel,
is dancing through the streets.
We try to avoid it
but it heads straight for us.
We reach for a clumsy last embrace
(better to die in each other's arms)—
are deposited on a lawn with other people.
A young woman is giving exercise classes.
Her name is Faux Primavera —
false spring.
I wake up laughing
and walk my mind like a stranger
wondering where the pain
is hiding.

14.

Death was on my mind that day.
I was writing blood on the page
but I was only dying by metaphors;
walking fields of midnight
with the hot fist of death in my hand.
It never occurred to me it could be real
until the sidewalk folded.
Each lovely street I turned into
thinking: Here I might die.
Dying of my own fault
in far-away Spain. Ludicrous
and useless.
Panic so real I *might* have died.

15.

My mind loose from its moorings.
Death lay its black weight on me again.
I ran to Trinidad Square.
Two elderly Americans and their middle-aged
son eating on the park bench, egg shells
falling at their feet.
At that moment the pressure mounted
to my head. Holding on in panic,
I thought: *In front of this*
prancing man and his irritated mother
who would rather be in Kansas!
The terror of falling off one's own mind.
I can imagine a fear so complete
it would be like crawling into a hole
and pulling the hole in after me.

16.

The wet light slips through the barred window.
Cold. Again all night, fear
like a hole in the heart.
Now the birds are pushing up light
from the earth. I put this fragile body-stocking
back on. Nothing so outrageous.

Something is dying
its slow protracted death.
I thought I left it behind
but I brought it with me.
I keep tearing away at the mystery:
this thing
I never had time to name.

17.

A white oasis in a green garden
against a blue and limpid sky.
The palace of the Alhambra turns inward,
its capitals carved on three sides only.
Despise the praise of admirers.

Above the window in the Hall of Sisters
the inscription: *How often
has that which was once very distant
come near! Happiness! Happiness!*
The ceiling a honeycomb of stone.
They have brought the firmament inside.
I push my face up
into the bin of stars.

I have reached the place to ask
why am I here. *You*
are beside the point. I am here
to meet myself.
If it weren't for this,
could there be a point?

And then
the strength to be *with*.

18.

If he finds no place for the heart,
she said, *he sickens.*
We keep reversing the drama.
You asleep. How am I to bring you
the thorn of myself?
I do not know whether I am a wall or a door?
Does it matter?
Enough to have lifted my life off its hinges.

I see now there is nothing for it
but love.

19.

I brought oranges to your bed.
It was five A.M.
That lovely Spanish word — the madrugada,
so tender: the sun sneaking back
over the earth.
You have read out the night.
You can only sleep in the light
after the sun walks in.
In your eyes, as we peel the skin
and suck the orange earth of Andalucia
I fall into the soft maze
of the madrugada.

20.

Come with me to the garden.
They are cooking the red peppers over slow braziers.
The earthen jars are gold with Moorish sun.
And they will tell us the secrets of water.
How it lifts and fills and falls as life does
in the inexorable diamond light.
You have to have been thirsty a long time
to know this much about water. Its cabala
of paths under the earth. How it thrusts up
in reluctant fistfuls. Here it falls
down handrails. We climb
holding the carved water in our hands.

21.

Someone called this a house,
though it is only a cave.
The porch and a rope survive.
Below in the Valley of Paradise
they are seeding the earth in tiers.
A cock crows.
A car announces the procession
from *Cristo* to *Jesus of the Sacred Corazón.*
Vecinos, the voice shouts.
On the wind the sweet thick smell
of olive oil cooking.
And the cacti like fish fins
cutting the air, a field of them,
with red fruit, prickled
and hairy as testicles.
Palm trees thrusting up from the landscape.
The day so sweet, and suddenly I turn
my head and at the end of the Valley of Paradise,
the white crest of the sierra.
How content you can be with the senses satisfied.
Birds loading the ear with their pleasures,
the eye framing a valley with mountains.
Is it yellow gorse on those hills?
The medusa trees not yet awake,
swinging their snake-like heads in the wind.
And I think this is enough:
To move past safety.
To be here now.
To live.